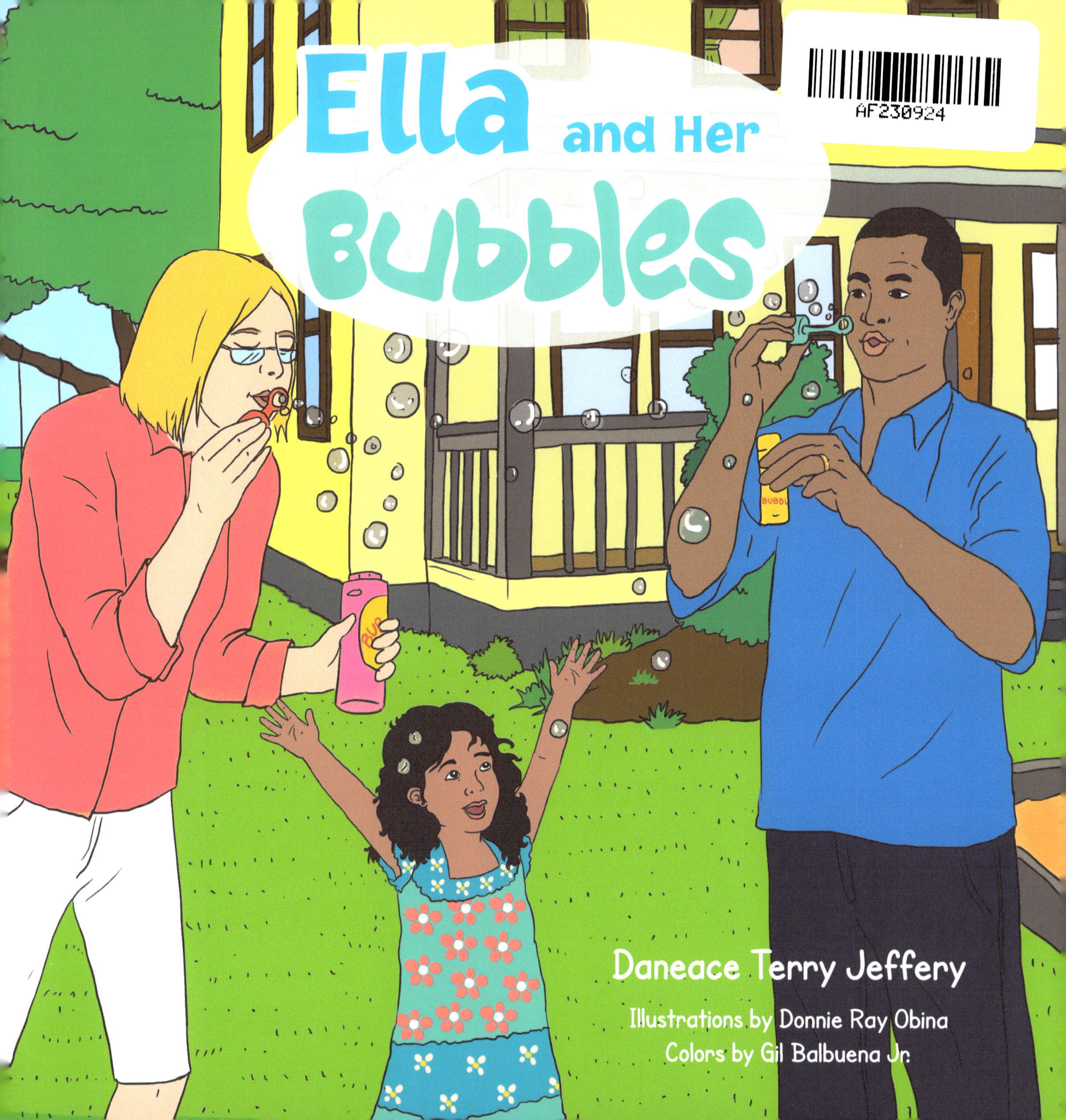

Ella and Her
Bubbles
Daneace Terry Jeffery
Illustrations by Donnie Ray Obina
Colors by Gil Balbuena Jr.
AF230924

Ella and Her Bubbles

By Daneace Terry Jeffery

Illustrations by Donnie Ray Obina
Colors by Gil Balbuena Jr.

My name is Ella and I am 3 years old. I like playing with balls, and dolls and all of my toys in our big backyard. I have lots of fun playing in the sandbox building sandcastles. But what I like most of all

is blowing bubbles on a summer day.

I like watching the bubbles float in the sky. Trying to catch bubbles with my hands and on my nose makes me giggle. Bubbles are so pretty in the sun. I like to see all the rainbow colors on the bubbles glistening in the sunlight. When the wind blows, bubbles fly even higher in the sky. My Mommy and Daddy take turns blowing bubbles for me.

But I want to blow bubbles all by myself!

6

One day Mommy tried to teach me how to blow my own
bubbles. But no matter how hard I tried, I couldn't do it. I
blew

        and blew

        and blew

        and blew,

          but…no bubbles.

Daddy said I had to blow on the wand very softly. So I tried to blow softly…but still no bubbles. Instead of blowing a bubble, I blew all the soap off the wand. It dripped all over my hands and dress.

10

Mommy says I can't blow the bubbles because I have too much soap on the wand. She tries to help me, but I want to do it myself. So I try again,

and again

and again,

but still…no bubbles.

625
12

When I went to visit Grandma Nonnie, she tried to teach me
how to slowly pull the wand out of the bottle. I tried to do
exactly as she said, but more soap ended up on the sides of
the bottle instead of on the wand. The outside of the bottle
became wet with soap and slipped right out of my hand and
splashed all over the steps. I started to cry, because now I
had no more bubbles to blow.

At Grandma Tammy's house, she told me to hold the wand away from my mouth and blow gently. I tried REALLY hard, again. But no bubbles with Grandma Tammy,

no bubbles with Daddy,

no bubbles with Mommy,

no bubbles with Grandma Nonnie.

I still don't know how to blow bubbles.

16

When Granddad came home from work; he saw that I was very sad. I had tried all day to learn how to blow bubbles. But I just couldn't do it. I tried to remember everything Daddy and Mommy told me. I tried to remember what Grandma Nonnie and Grandma Tammy told me. Then Granddad said he had an idea.

18

Granddad picked a white dandelion flower from the backyard and gently blew on it. The white petals began to float in the wind just like bubbles. Granddad then taught me how to hold the wand just like the dandelion flower.

Granddad told me to try one more time. And this time, I remembered everything my family taught me. I held the wand just right. I blew on the wand just right. And then it happened.

I BLEW A BUBBLE!

And then another,

and another

and another!

Yippee, I was blowing bubbles all by myself, thanks to my family.

Now, I can blow my own bubbles wherever I go.